Little People, **BIG DREAMS**

AUDREY HEPBURN

Written by
Mª Isabel Sánchez Vegara

Illustrated by
Amaia Arrazola

Frances Lincoln
Children's Books

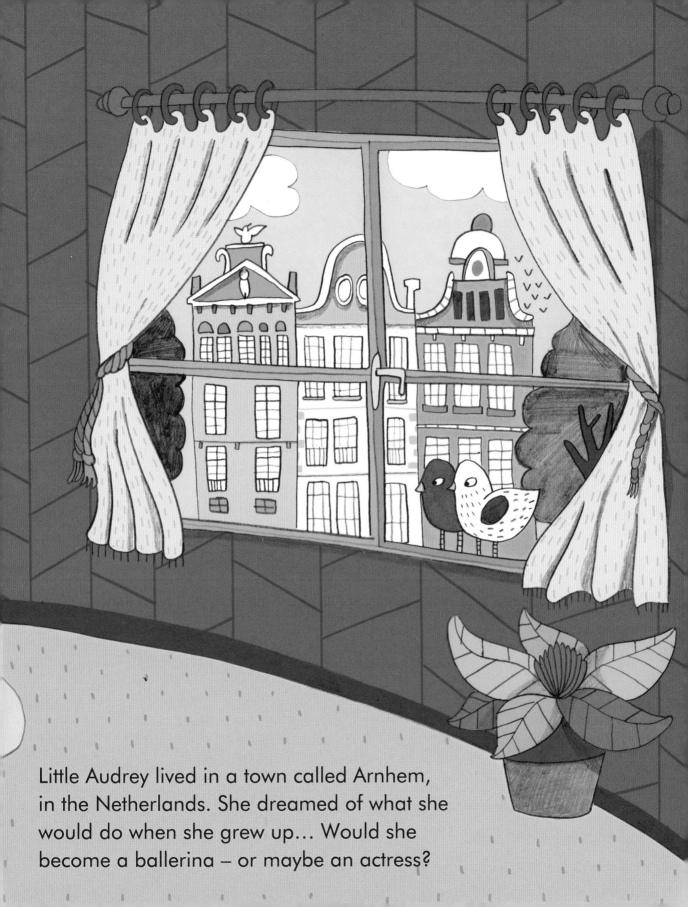

Little Audrey lived in a town called Arnhem, in the Netherlands. She dreamed of what she would do when she grew up... Would she become a ballerina – or maybe an actress?

But one day, on her way to ballet
class, Audrey saw soldiers on the
streets. War had broken out. She watched
many families being sent away from their homes –
including children just like her.

It was a hard time for Audrey and all the other children. There was very little food and they were often hungry. Audrey became very ill.

At last the fighting ended, and Audrey moved to London to study dance. Her teacher said she was too weak from the war to become a ballerina. But Audrey didn't give up...

She decided to act and dance in musicals instead!

Before long, she was making her first Hollywood film – driving around Rome with the famous actor, Gregory Peck!

Every role she played was different from the one before.
One day she was a nun, and the next... a princess!

She had a simple rule for life: 'Dance as though no one is watching. Sing as though no one can hear you. Live as though heaven is on Earth'.

She also liked to spend time alone in her apartment. Every day at breakfast, she read letters from her fans. She was loved by millions of people around the world!

Audrey won award after award. But she worried that she didn't deserve them. Whilst she was a Hollywood star who seemed to have everything...

She never forgot that there were children in the world who were hungry, just like she had been.

One day, a charity offered her a new role. They asked her to become their official ambassador and visit children all over the world! So Audrey travelled to India…

… and to Africa! Wherever she went, Audrey tried to make every child happy. She helped raise money to provide children with water, food and medicine.

Audrey spent the rest of her life helping
people across the globe. And that made her
happier than acting or dancing ever had.

AUDREY HEPBURN

(Born 1929 • Died 1993)

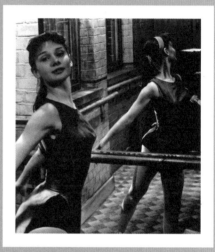

1946 (right)   1950

Audrey Hepburn was one of the most iconic actresses of stage
and screen. She was born Audrey Kathleen Ruston in Belgium,
in 1929. Her mother, Ella van Heemstra, was a Dutch baroness
and her father, Joseph Ruston, was British. Her parents broke up
when she was three and Audrey moved with her mother to
Arnhem, a small town in the Netherlands. It was here that
Audrey started to take ballet lessons. When World War Two
broke out in 1939, Audrey's mother hoped that the Netherlands
would be safe. Unfortunately Audrey's family, like many others,
suffered greatly during the war. Food was scarce and she
witnessed crimes she would remember for the rest of her life.

1956

1991

After the war, Audrey trained to be a ballerina, moving to London to study at the famous Rambert School of Ballet. But she was weak from years of malnutrition, so she decided to focus on acting instead of ballet. She got her big break in the Broadway play *Gigi*, and went on to star in many Hollywood films, such as *Breakfast at Tiffany's*, winning prestigious awards. During her retirement, the children's charity UNICEF asked her to be their Goodwill Ambassador. She travelled all around the world, raising awareness for children who needed food, clean water and medicine. Audrey did whatever she could to help others, because she remembered how she had felt when she was a child in need.

Want to find out more about **Audrey Hepburn**?

Have a read of this great book:

Just Being Audrey by Margaret Cardillo

You could also watch one of her many films, such as *My Fair Lady* or *Roman Holiday*.

Brimming with creative inspiration, how-to projects, and useful information to enrich your everyday life, Quarto Knows is a favourite destination for those pursuing their interests and passions. Visit our site and dig deeper with our books into your area of interest: Quarto Creates, Quarto Cooks, Quarto Homes, Quarto Lives, Quarto Drives, Quarto Explores, Quarto Gifts, or Quarto Kids.

Inspiring | Educating | Creating | Entertaining

First published in the UK in 2017 by Lincoln Children's Books,
an imprint of The Quarto Group, The Old Brewery, 6 Blundell Street, London N7 9BH QuartoKnows.com
Visit our blogs at QuartoKids.com

Text copyright © 2015 by Mª Isabel Sánchez Vegara
Illustrations copyright © 2015 by Amaia Arrazola

First published in Spain in 2015 under the title *Pequeña & Grande Audrey Hepburn*
by Alba Editorial, s.l.u., Baixada de Sant Miquel, 1, 08002 Barcelona
www.albaeditorial.es

A catalogue record for this book is available from the British Library.

ISBN 978-1-78603-052-8

Published by Rachel Williams • Designed by Karissa Santos
Edited by Katy Flint • Production by Kate O'Riordan
Manufactured in Guangdong, China CC072019

MIX
Paper from responsible sources
FSC
www.fsc.org
FSC® C008047

Photographic acknowledgements (pages 28-29, from left to right) 1. Audrey Hepburn with mother, 1946 © Hulton Archive, Getty Images 2. Audrey Hepburn rehearsing at the barre, 1950 © Silver Screen Collection, Getty Images 3. Audrey Hepburn in Funny Face, 1956 © Mondadori Portfolio, Getty Images 4. UNICEF Gala honouring Audrey Hepburn, 1991 © Ron Galella, Getty Images

Collect the *Little People,* **BIG DREAMS** series:

FRIDA KAHLO

ISBN: 978-1-84780-770-0

COCO CHANEL

ISBN: 978-1-84780-771-7

MAYA ANGELOU

ISBN: 978-1-84780-890-5

AMELIA EARHART

ISBN: 978-1-84780-885-1

AGATHA CHRISTIE

ISBN: 978-1-84780-959-9

MARIE CURIE

ISBN: 978-1-84780-961-2

ROSA PARKS

ISBN: 978-1-78603-017-7

AUDREY HEPBURN

ISBN: 978-1-78603-052-8

EMMELINE PANKHURST

ISBN: 978-1-78603-019-1

ELLA FITZGERALD

ISBN: 978-1-78603-086-3

ADA LOVELACE

ISBN: 978-1-78603-075-7

JANE AUSTEN

ISBN: 978-1-78603-119-8

GEORGIA O'KEEFFE

ISBN: 978-1-78603-121-1

HARRIET TUBMAN
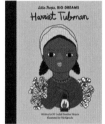
ISBN: 978-1-78603-289-8

ANNE FRANK

ISBN: 978-1-78603-292-8

MOTHER TERESA

ISBN: 978-1-78603-290-4

JOSEPHINE BAKER

ISBN: 978-1-78603-291-1

L. M. MONTGOMERY

ISBN: 978-1-78603-295-9

JANE GOODALL

ISBN: 978-1-78603-294-2

SIMONE DE BEAUVOIR

ISBN: 978-1-78603-293-5

Now in board book format:

COCO CHANEL

ISBN: 978-1-78603-246-1

MAYA ANGELOU

ISBN: 978-1-78603-250-8

FRIDA KAHLO

ISBN: 978-1-78603-248-5

AMELIA EARHART

ISBN: 978-1-78603-251-5

MARIE CURIE

ISBN: 978-1-78603-254-6